Farshore

First published in Great Britain 2021 by Farshore
An imprint of HarperCollins*Publishers*
1 London Bridge Street, London SE1 9GF
www.farshore.co.uk

HarperCollins*Publishers*
1st Floor, Watermarque Building, Ringsend Road
Dublin 04, Ireland

Written by Dan Whitehead
Edited by Thomas McBrien
Illustrated by Ryan Marsh
Designed by Paul Lang
Special thanks to Sherin Kwan, Alex Wiltshire, Kelsey Howard and Milo Bengtsson

This book is an original creation by Farshore
© 2021 HarperCollins*Publishers* Limited

ISBN 978 0 7555 0107 6
Printed in Romania
004

ONLINE SAFETY FOR YOUNGER FANS

Spending time online is great fun! Here are a few simple rules to help younger fans stay safe and
keep the internet a great place to spend time:
- Never give out your real name – don't use it as your username.
- Never give out any of your personal details.
- Never tell anybody which school you go to or how old you are.
- Never tell anybody your password except a parent or a guardian.
- Be aware that you must be 13 or over to create an account on many sites.
Always check the site policy and ask a parent or guardian for permission before registering.
- Always tell a parent or guardian if something is worrying you.

Stay safe online. Any website addresses listed in this book are correct at the time of going to print.
However, Farshore is not responsible for content hosted by third parties. Please be aware that online content
can be subject to change and websites can contain content that is unsuitable for children.
We advise that all children are supervised when using the internet.

Stay safe online. Farshore is not responsible for content hosted by third parties.

MIX
Paper from
responsible sources
FSC™ C007454

MINECRAFT

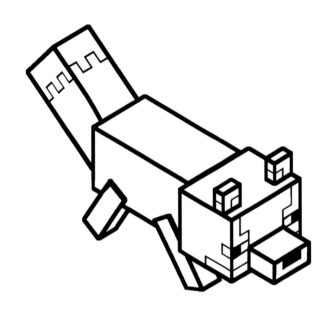

ANNUAL 2022

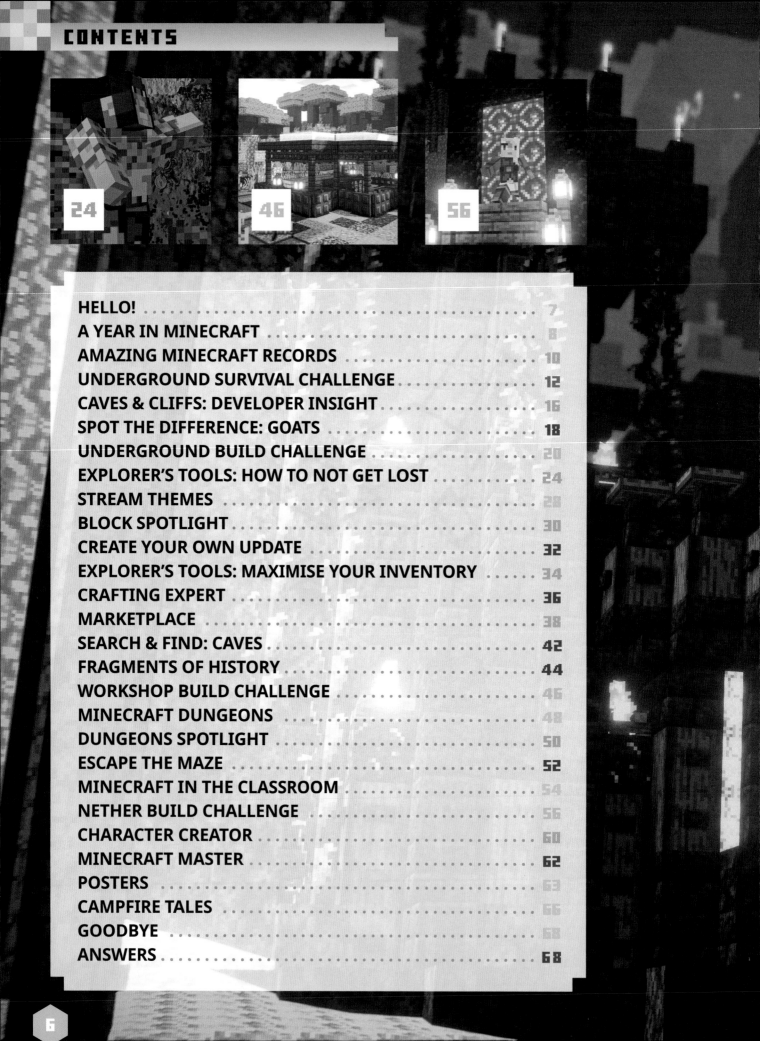

CONTENTS

HELLO!

Welcome to the Minecraft Annual 2022! I don't know about you, but this year has gone in a flash! Maybe it was because I spent so much of it underground and didn't notice the days going by ...

Anyway, it's great to get a chance to look back over it! We'll be looking at how Minecraft has been used to teach about the brave visionaries who led the Civil Rights Movement in the United States, and also to explore ways that humans and animals can live together more harmoniously.

Of course we'll delve deep into Minecraft's new underworld, which released this year in the form of the Caves & Cliffs update! It sure is full of the weird (and cute, if we're talking axolotls) and wonderful (amethyst geodes!).

We'll explore some of the DLC packs that have been added to *Minecraft Dungeons*, which span the Nether,

the jungle and the frozen wastes. By the way, how are you getting on with Apocalypse Plus?

We'll also showcase what our wonderful community has been doing, from amazing adventure maps and texture packs on Marketplace to an incredible ongoing attempt to construct the entire world in the game.

All these things bring together what's special about Minecraft: it's a place for exploration and discovery, and imagination and storytelling, and people coming together to build things, learn, and share ideas.

And it wouldn't be any of these things without you. It's great you've come with us on the ride! Let's go!

Alex Wiltshire
MOJANG STUDIOS

A YEAR IN MINECRAFT

There's no such thing as a quiet year in Minecraft – there's always something happening, and this year is no different! From Nintendo crossovers to globetrotting players, here are some of this year's highlights that caught our eye.

BABY YODA
It's been over five years since the first Star Wars skin pack arrived in 2014, so this year's addition of an all-new map, textures and characters – including *The Mandalorian's* cutest baby – was a real treat!

GOATS!
These mischievous creatures enjoy nothing more than knocking players backwards!

VIRTUAL REALITY
PlayStation owners could finally get inside the game in eye-popping virtual reality thanks to the free PSVR update. Look out behind you!

SQUID'S IN!
The groovy glow squid from *Minecraft Earth* was voted by players to be the first mob from a spin-off to be added to the base game!

SMASHING!
The crossovers got crazy when Steve and Alex joined Mario and friends in the line-up of fighters for *Super Smash Bros Ultimate!*

CHANGE THE WORLD

Minecraft has been helping to bring about change in the real world too, and raised $2.15M for important social justice projects! Among the projects launched was *Good Trouble: Lessons in Social Justice*, that went live in November 2020. Learn how "good trouble" encouraged people to speak up and challenge injustice on page 55.

GLOBAL GAMING

Minecraft was enjoyed by players in every single country on the planet this year. It was even played in Antarctica!

ICEOLOGERS!

This frosty new illager from *Minecraft Dungeons* drops blocks of ice on your head! Chill out, mate!

DUNGEONS FOR ALL

Minecraft Dungeons allowed everyone to play together regardless of platform thanks to a free cross-play update!

LET'S ROCK!

The Caves & Cliffs update added loads of new features to the game, including precious amethyst shards!

PIGLIN BRUTES

What's that? You wanted even tougher mobs in the game? OK, you asked for it! The axe-wielding piglin brute will test even the strongest warrior!

A WHOLE LOTTA AXOLOTL

Perhaps the cutest critter ever to swim in Minecraft waters, the colourful little axolotl can be collected in buckets!

AMAZING MINECRAFT RECORDS

EXPERT GUIDE
WITH SPARKS

The amazing Minecraft community keeps coming up with wild new ways to set world records. Some of these record holders have retained their title for years! Reckon you can beat any of these and claim a record for yourself?

FIRST GAME COMPLETION USING A PIANO

YouTuber Jachael123 not only hooked up an actual musical keyboard to their computer and programmed it as a Minecraft controller, they actually beat the game in seven and a half hours using this bizarre method! Yep, that includes defeating the ender dragon! Skilful and tuneful – amazing work!

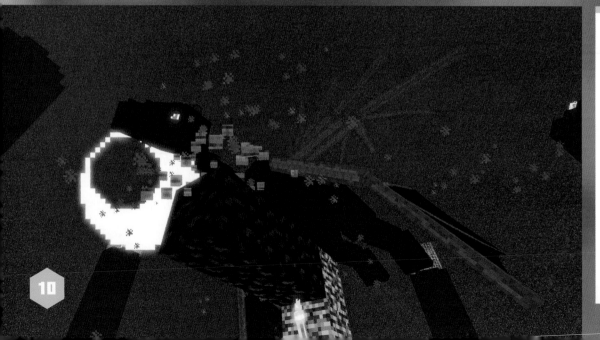

FASTEST SPEEDRUN OF ALL TIME

In August 2020 MinecrAvenger set a new record for the fastest completion of the game, doing so in just 3 minutes and 6 seconds. What was their secret? They spawned near a village, stole all the beds and used them as explosives in the End! Since then, other speedrunners have beaten the record using the same strategy.

MOST STEVES!

337 visitors at MineVention, a 2015 fan event in Peterborough, all dressed up as Minecraft's legendary hero to claim the official world record for the most Steves in one place!

FIRST TO REACH THE FAR LANDS

It took YouTuber KilloCrazyMan nine long months to walk on foot to the Far Lands, becoming the first person to reach the edge of Minecraft's world without teleporting or cheating the strange glitched edge of the world that existed in older versions of Java Edition. He arrived at his destination after walking a massive 12.5 million blocks from his spawn point. If you play Java Edition, don't try to follow in his footsteps because you'll be walking forever! But they still exist in Bedrock Edition ...

LONGEST EVER HARDCORE SURVIVAL GAME

British YouTuber Phil "Philza" Watson managed to stay alive for an astonishing five years in a single Hardcore Survival game, streaming his daring adventure several times a week. In the end, he was undone by a baby zombie wearing enchanted armour. What a way to go!

LONGEST MARATHON!

Mark Walls-Sawchuck played Minecraft non-stop for 35 hours, 40 minutes, 2 seconds for a charity stream, earning the world record for the longest Minecraft marathon.

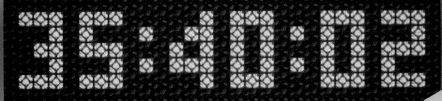

UNDERGROUND SURVIVAL CHALLENGE

Underground caves and canyons can be unforgiving places, filled with endless passages, precipitous falls and dangerous mobs. Surviving can be a real challenge for even top Minecrafters, so let's put your skills to the test! Complete each of these steps and see how long you can survive underground before returning to the surface.

1 GATHER SUPPLIES

It's vital to prepare before venturing underground. Gather the supplies you will need to survive, especially if they can't be found underground. Be sure to include food, water, saplings, seeds and dirt – they will be vital for your continued survival.

2 CRAFT YOUR EQUIPMENT

Did you know a creeper can instantly kill an unarmoured player? That's why you need to craft some equipment before encountering dangerous mobs. Wearing a basic set of armour will help to keep you from an untimely death. Don't forget a sword!

3 PREPARE YOUR PICKAXE

Prepare yourself for life underground with a few iron pickaxes. You can even create an enchantment table and enchant your pickaxe with both Efficiency and Unbreaking to increase your mining speed and item durability.

DEFEAT THE MOB HORDE

5 As you climb deeper and deeper underground, get ready to defend yourself from the zombies, skeletons and spiders intent on seeing you fall. Listen for the sound of nearby mobs, and if you see a mob spawner, get ready to fight for your life!

FIND A MINESHAFT

4 It's time to make your way underground! Locate a nearby cave or mineshaft, equip a stack of torches and embark on a journey to the depths of the Overworld. Place a trail of signs behind you as you descend underground so you can retrace your footsteps to the exit later.

LOCATE A LARGE CAVERN

6 Continue venturing deeper underground until you find a large, tall cavern suitable for a base. Prepare the cavern by lighting it up with torches and clearing out any remaining mobs. Remember to place a sign to point out the exit.

UNDERGROUND SURVIVAL CHALLENGE

PART 2

7 TEMPORARY SHELTER

Next, build yourself a temporary shelter in the cavern. The structure doesn't need to be complicated – four walls, a door, a roof and a few torches will do the job. Sleep in a bed to save your respawn point and store your supplies in chests.

8 ELIXIR OF LIFE

By now your resources are starting to dwindle. It's time to prepare more supplies for the days ahead! First, create an infinite water source using two buckets of water placed two blocks apart. Fill your bucket using the middle water block.

9 FARMING FOR THE FUTURE

Next, grab your stacks of dirt from the supply chest and use them to create a large underground field for farming. Check that the cavern has high ceilings and is well-lit, and use your infinite water supply to keep the farmland watered.

10 · SEEDS FOR SUSTENANCE

Once your farmland is ready for planting, collect the seeds from your supply chest and start planting crops. Plant a variety of seeds like melons, beetroot and wheat to ensure a balanced diet. Make sure the farm is well-lit for your crops to grow!

11 · CAVERN COPSE

Next, you're going to need to replenish your supply of wood. Using your tree saplings, return to the underground farmland and plant a small forest of sustainable trees. It is vital that the cavern has tall ceilings for the trees to grow.

12 · SURVIVE!

You're now all set up with everything you need to survive underground. How long will you last before returning to the surface? Continue to upgrade your shelter as you strive to survive for as long as possible without returning to the surface.

CAVES & CLIFFS: DEVELOPER INSIGHT

The Caves and Cliffs update has hit the main stage, and it's a big one. With so much new content, we simply had to hear more about how the dev team was inspired. We asked Nir "Ulraf" Vaknin, one of the gameplay developers working on the update, to share some developer insights on these popular new additions to the game.

COPPER

"Adding a new ore is very big for Minecraft."

New ores pose fresh challenges, as they've got to be just right for the game. Copper was no different, with unique challenges like the new oxidising game mechanic, which causes the block to turn green over time.

"It was really hard to design the length of time the transition would take."

Too short and blocks would change too quickly, or too long and players could feel frustrated with the wait. It was a Minecraft Goldilocks puzzle – not too hot and not too cold; it had to be just right.

LIGHTNING ROD

"We have a design directive that if something bad happens, it must either be because of something the player has done, or something the player can avoid. Lightning has broken this directive."

This became clear to Nir one sunny afternoon in Minecraft: he was returning from an adventure only to find half his base had been destroyed by lightning. Although it wasn't his fault, he still felt pretty lousy about it. Needless to say, this is not how Mojang want players to feel, so it was decided a solution was needed. This rod solves the issue by attracting and grounding the lighning strikes.

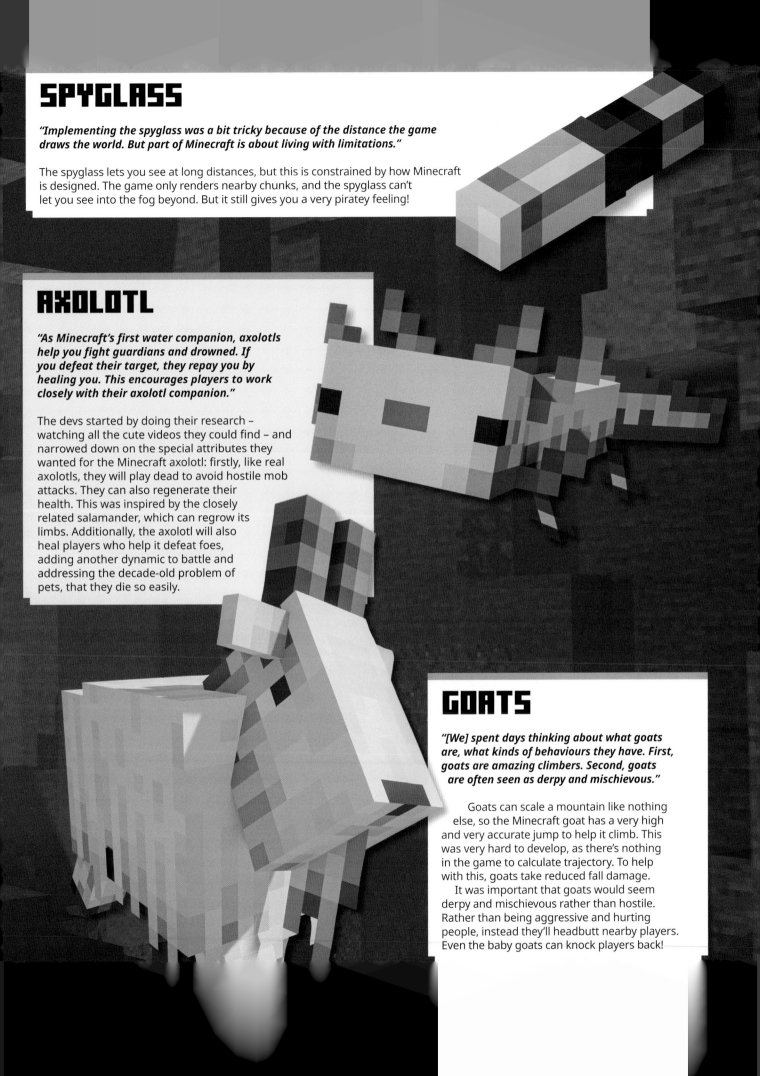

SPYGLASS

"Implementing the spyglass was a bit tricky because of the distance the game draws the world. But part of Minecraft is about living with limitations."

The spyglass lets you see at long distances, but this is constrained by how Minecraft is designed. The game only renders nearby chunks, and the spyglass can't let you see into the fog beyond. But it still gives you a very piratey feeling!

AXOLOTL

"As Minecraft's first water companion, axolotls help you fight guardians and drowned. If you defeat their target, they repay you by healing you. This encourages players to work closely with their axolotl companion."

The devs started by doing their research – watching all the cute videos they could find – and narrowed down on the special attributes they wanted for the Minecraft axolotl: firstly, like real axolotls, they will play dead to avoid hostile mob attacks. They can also regenerate their health. This was inspired by the closely related salamander, which can regrow its limbs. Additionally, the axolotl will also heal players who help it defeat foes, adding another dynamic to battle and addressing the decade-old problem of pets, that they die so easily.

GOATS

"[We] spent days thinking about what goats are, what kinds of behaviours they have. First, goats are amazing climbers. Second, goats are often seen as derpy and mischievous."

Goats can scale a mountain like nothing else, so the Minecraft goat has a very high and very accurate jump to help it climb. This was very hard to develop, as there's nothing in the game to calculate trajectory. To help with this, goats take reduced fall damage.

It was important that goats would seem derpy and mischievous rather than hostile. Rather than being aggressive and hurting people, instead they'll headbutt nearby players. Even the baby goats can knock players back!

SPOT THE DIFFERENCE
GOAT

CHALLENGE
TIME
WITH BEAR

Reports have reached us of a new mob seen roaming the tops of mountains. Keen to learn more, players have attempted to scale the mountain to reach them, only to be knocked back down! Undismayed, players have taken out their spyglasses to take a look. Can you spot the 10 differences between these two goats?

1 ◯ 2 ◯ 3 ⬡ 4 ◯ 5 ◯ 6 ◯ 7 ⬡ 8 ⬡ 9 ◯ 10 ◯

Check your answers on page 68

UNDERGROUND BUILD CHALLENGE

BUILDING
WITH SPARKS

Spending days and weeks deep beneath the ground, far from the sun, can test the mettle of any adventurer. With danger lurking around every corner, an underground base must be ready for all possible threats. Preparing for such treacherous living conditions is no easy task — are you up for the challenge?

2 BELLS
Alarm bells are a great way to keep your base safe. Connect tripwires to bells in each of the passages leading into and out of the cavern – the bells will ring whenever an intruder enters. If you hear a bell ring, grab your sword and get ready to defend your home!

1 LIVING SPACE
First you must venture deep below ground and find a large cavern in which to build your base. A large, spacious cavern will help you keep organised and allow you to spot danger from far away.

3 LIGHT IT UP
Light up the entire cavern with torches and other light sources, even inside neighbouring tunnels and passages. Make sure there are no dark corners for mobs to spawn in and surprise you.

4 IRON FORTRESS
At the heart of the cavern, build a strongroom using iron blocks, an iron door and fenced windows. Should your base be overrun with hordes of mobs, this strongroom will keep you safe until the threat has passed.

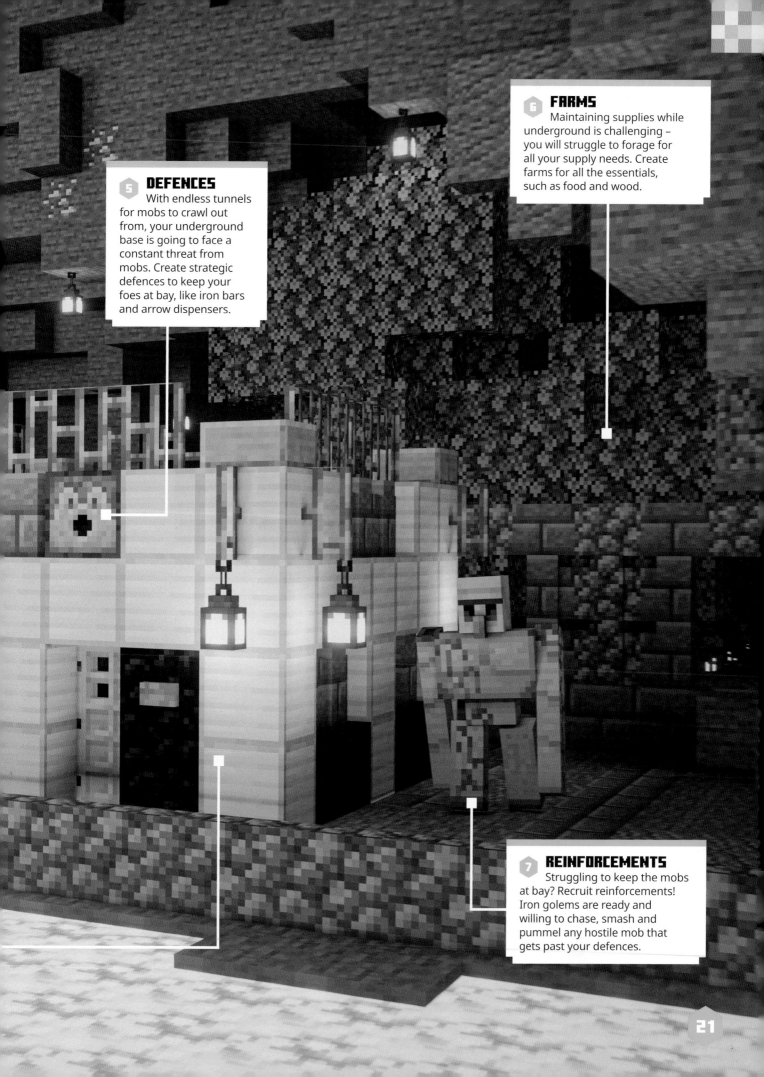

5 DEFENCES

With endless tunnels for mobs to crawl out from, your underground base is going to face a constant threat from mobs. Create strategic defences to keep your foes at bay, like iron bars and arrow dispensers.

6 FARMS

Maintaining supplies while underground is challenging – you will struggle to forage for all your supply needs. Create farms for all the essentials, such as food and wood.

7 REINFORCEMENTS

Struggling to keep the mobs at bay? Recruit reinforcements! Iron golems are ready and willing to chase, smash and pummel any hostile mob that gets past your defences.

UNDERGROUND BUILD CHALLENGE

PART 2

BUILDING
WITH SPARKS

STURDIER MATERIALS

Zombies will stop at nothing to reach a player – wooden doors won't hold them back for long! To stay safe, you're going to need to build your strongroom with sturdier materials. An iron fortress with an iron door is sure to keep mobs at bay.

LOOKOUT

Build lookout slots and defensive features into your strongroom. A lava dispenser by the door will clear away hammering mobs, while the viewing slots will let you know when it's safe to step out.

IRON STRONGROOM STRUCTURE

🕒 **0.5 HRS**　◆◆◆◇ **MODERATE**

Building an impenetrable strongroom will keep you prepared for anything and everything. Whether it's a horde of angry mobs or a flood of lava, if ever your life is put in danger, you can step into this iron strongroom and wait it out.

BUILD TIP

Remember to add buttons for the iron door both inside and outside the strongroom to avoid getting locked in, or worse, locked out!

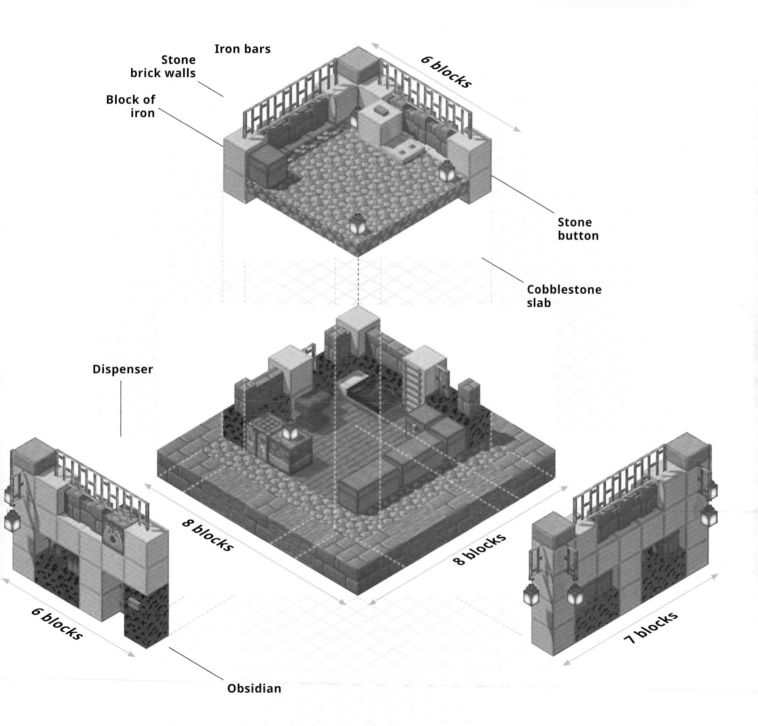

Iron bars

Stone brick walls

Block of iron

6 blocks

Stone button

Cobblestone slab

Dispenser

8 blocks

8 blocks

6 blocks

7 blocks

Obsidian

EXPLORER'S TOOLS:
HOW NOT TO GET LOST

EXPERT GUIDE WITH BEAR

Have you ever wandered too far from home following a cute rabbit, or delved too deep into a dungeon and found yourself hopelessly lost? You're not the only one! For years, players have been retracing their footsteps to find lost bases and mineshafts.
To deal with this common issue, we've decided to share our top tips to not get lost.

1 SET A RESPAWN LOCATION

The quickest, easiest and surest way to ensure you never lose your beloved base is to set up a respawn point. To do so, place a bed and click on it to sleep. Then, if you ever die, you will spawn again back at home.

2 SAVE YOUR COORDINATES

A guaranteed way to never forget where you built your base is to keep a note of its coordinates. Press F3 or select the coordinates option in the menu to find your exact location, then simply navigate towards it whenever you get lost.

3 BREADCRUMB TRAIL

If you like to set out on faraway adventures then this next trick is just for you. When you embark on your adventure, prepare stacks of torches and leave a breadcrumb trail of them behind you. To return home, follow the torches back to the source.

4 NATURAL LANDMARKS

A great tool for not getting lost is to study nearby landmarks. Explore the area and make a note of the distinctive features you see, like pillager outposts and villages. These will help you quickly identify where you are and which direction you need to go.

5 BLOCK TOWERS & CAMPFIRE SIGNALS

You can also create your own landmarks to help identify an area, like block towers and campfire signals. These landmarks are visible from a great distance and will provide markers to help you navigate.

6 BEACONS

The most effective handmade landmark you can create is a beacon. Beacons will shine a bright light directly into the sky and are visible from great distances. Plus, they give you bonus stats, like speed and jump boosts. However, they require a lot of resources to create.

EXPLORER'S TOOLS:
HOW NOT TO GET LOST

7 CARDINAL DIRECTIONS

You can use traditional methods to never get lost. With the understanding that the sun and moon rise in the east and set in the west, that clouds always travel westward and that stars turn anticlockwise, you can navigate any direction without a compass.

8 MAPS & COMPASSES

Alternatively, you can use a map and compass to navigate and explore an area while creating a visual map to help you remember. The map will record everything you see, like structures and rivers. It will even update if you add or remove blocks.

9 BANNERS & LANDMARKS

Banners and landmarks are a great way to save information about the surrounding area. If you play Java Edition, click a map on a banner to save a location and use different colour banners for different purposes. If you play Bedrock Edition, create copies of locator maps and place them in frames to create landmarks.

🔟 WORLD MAP

As you explore further and further out, you will fill more and more maps of the surrounding biomes. You can use these maps to create a world map display board. Use item frames to create a billboard and slot each map into place. It's just like completing a jigsaw, except it's your world.

1️⃣1️⃣ LODESTONE

Lodestones are naturally magnetised minerals that can interact with compasses. If you find a lodestone, bring it to your base and use a compass on it. This will cause the needle to point toward the lodestone, giving you a compass that always points home. Handy for finding the most direct route back to base.

STREAM THEMES

With millions of active users worldwide, it's no surprise that Minecraft is one of the most popular games to stream online. But as a sandbox game, there's no set way to play the game. So, what are Minecrafters streaming? More importantly: What are Minecrafters watching?

1 MINECRAFT LIVE

The show that all Minecrafters know and love – Minecraft Live. Tune in once a year to discover the latest news in the world of Minecraft, including upcoming releases and voting on the next new mob! This is the place to go for all the latest Mojang news. Millions of viewers tune in each year!

2 LET'S PLAY

In this stream theme, streamers begin with a new Survival world and complete a series of projects from scratch. Streamers provide commentary and interact with fans as they explore and create new builds over the course of many weeks.

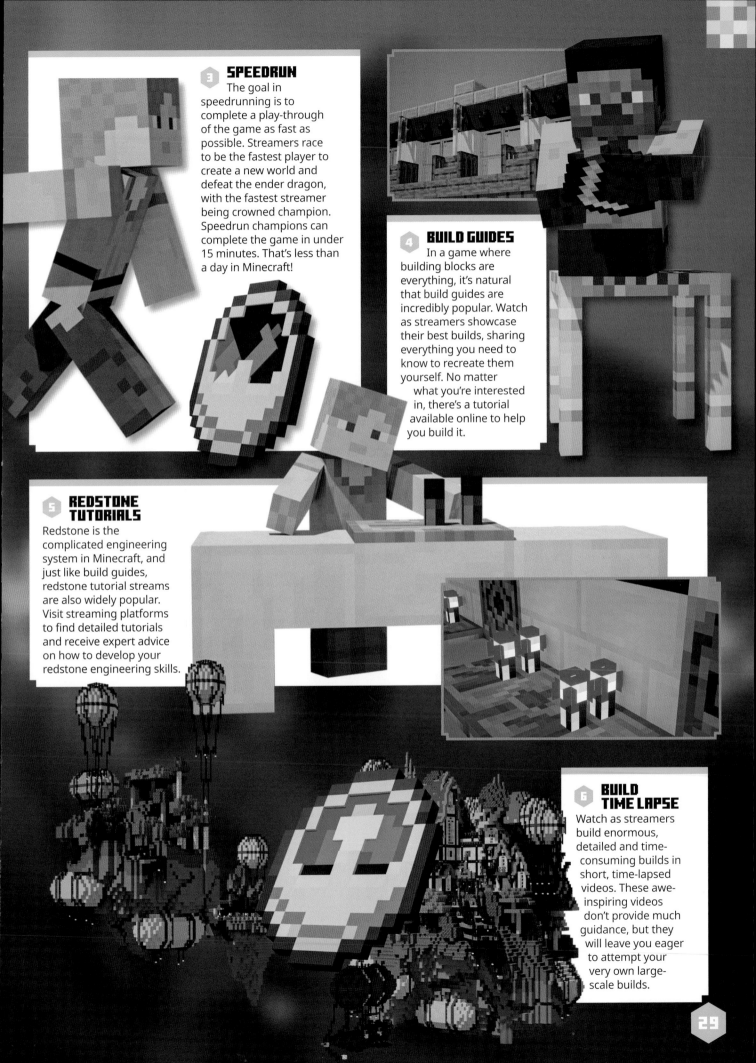

SPEEDRUN

The goal in speedrunning is to complete a play-through of the game as fast as possible. Streamers race to be the fastest player to create a new world and defeat the ender dragon, with the fastest streamer being crowned champion. Speedrun champions can complete the game in under 15 minutes. That's less than a day in Minecraft!

BUILD GUIDES

In a game where building blocks are everything, it's natural that build guides are incredibly popular. Watch as streamers showcase their best builds, sharing everything you need to know to recreate them yourself. No matter what you're interested in, there's a tutorial available online to help you build it.

REDSTONE TUTORIALS

Redstone is the complicated engineering system in Minecraft, and just like build guides, redstone tutorial streams are also widely popular. Visit streaming platforms to find detailed tutorials and receive expert advice on how to develop your redstone engineering skills.

BUILD TIME LAPSE

Watch as streamers build enormous, detailed and time-consuming builds in short, time-lapsed videos. These awe-inspiring videos don't provide much guidance, but they will leave you eager to attempt your very own large-scale builds.

BLOCK SPOTLIGHT

EXPERT GUIDE
WITH MONTY

Did you know that there are over 600 unique blocks in Minecraft? That's a lot of blocks. There weren't always this many. Every year, Mojang add more and more blocks with more and more functions for players to enjoy. They've added over 40 this year alone! Let's take a look at some of the cool things they do.

COPPER ORE

Copper is a new ore block. Its ores can make copper blocks, the first block that changes appearance over time. Copper is available in four variant forms, and copper ingots can be used to create helpful items, such as telescopes and lightning rods.

POWDER SNOW

A.K.A. 'snowier snow', this new snow block is just like regular snow except that entities can fall through it. You can collect it in snowy biomes with a cauldron. Watch out! If you get stuck in powder snow for too long, you'll freeze and start to take damage.

ROOTED DIRT

Keep an eye out for azalea plants as you explore. Their roots have introduced a new strategy for finding resources. Simply following the rooted dirt will lead you through the ground to a lush cave. What a cool new way to explore!

BLOCK OF AMETHYST

Minecrafters love textures and sounds – just look at how many blocks and music discs there are! So it's no surprise that we also love the block of amethyst. This purple block looks incredible, and even makes a quiet chiming sound when you walk on it.

CAVE VINES

This new block is a light source, a food source and even, when used creatively, a building block. With so much versatility, it promises to become a regular feature in community builds. I've always wanted to try food that glows.

BIG DRIPLEAF

The big dripleaf is the newest plant to find in-game. This special block grows both on land and in water and has a little platform you can stand on. Unlike other plants, if you stand on it for too long the leaf will tilt and make you fall.

TINTED GLASS

Although it's scary in the dark, we simply had to include tinted glass in our selection. You can see through this special block, but it blocks all light. With light being the nemesis of mobs, we're certain this block will redefine how mob farms are built.

LIGHTNING ROD

Though this block might reignite sore memories of burned down builds, many will be excited to hear about the new lightning rod. Place one of these on your structure to divert lightning strikes and turn them into redstone signals.

CREATE YOUR OWN UPDATE

From the Update that Changed the World to Buzzy Bees and now Caves & Cliffs, Minecraft has undergone dozens of transformations to become the game it is today. Devs have put countless hours into creating fun, exciting content for eager fans, and now it's your turn! If you could create your own update, what would you do?

DESCRIBE YOUR UPDATE

Name: ....

Description: ....

....

....

CREATE YOUR NEW MOB

Name: ....

♥ ♥ ♥ ♥ ♥

Name: ....

♥ ♥ ♥ ♥ ♥

Describe your mob: ....

....

....

Describe your mob: ....

....

....

DESIGN YOUR NEW BLOCKS

Name: . . . .

Name: . . . .

Name: . . . .

Name: . . . .

CRAFT YOUR NEW ITEMS

Name: . . . .

Name: . . . .

Name: . . . .

Describe your item:

. . . .

. . . .

Describe your item:

. . . .

. . . .

Describe your item:

. . . .

. . . .

EXPLORER'S TOOLS:
MAXIMISE YOUR INVENTORY

EXPERT GUIDE WITH MONTY

Imagine this: You're deep underground, far from your base, and you have just found a big cluster of diamond ores — except you're out of inventory space! We've all been there, trying to decide what items to keep and to leave behind. It's a tough situation, but have you maximised your inventory? Let's find out.

1 BLOCK STACKS

Check that you're maximising your stack space. Ore stacks can have 64 units, but did you know you can smelt ores into ingots and then combine ingots into blocks? Using this trick, you can turn 576 ingots into just one stack of 64 blocks! Use the same trick for other minerals such as coal, redstone dust and lapis lazuli.

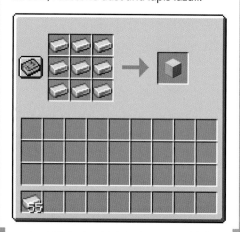

2 SHULKER CHEST

Sometimes when you embark on a long journey you need to carry lots of supplies, leaving you with little remaining inventory. Shulker chests are a great solution. First, place a shulker chest and fill it with blocks. Then break the chest and pick it up – when you place it again, all the blocks will be there waiting for you.

3 ENDER CHEST

Did you know that every ender chest is connected? Place an ender chest in your base and keep a spare ender chest in your inventory. When you run out of inventory space, place the spare chest and fill it with resources. They will be available in your base when you return. There's 27 slots to fill, so it's best used for your most valuable items.

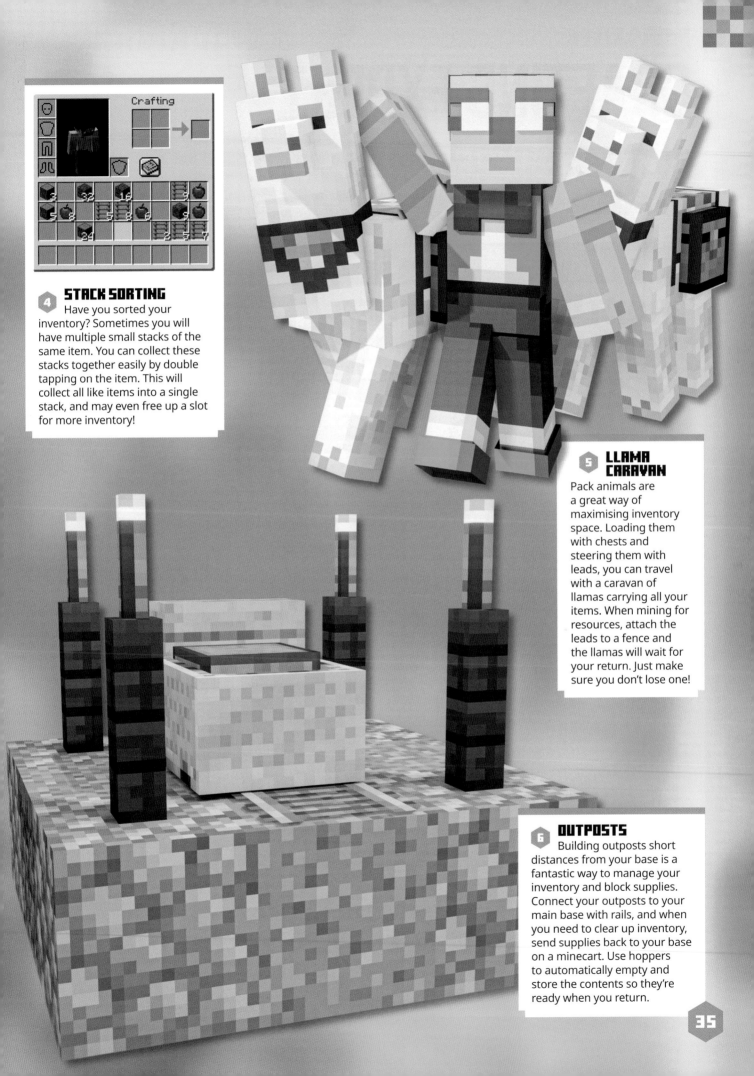

4 STACK SORTING

Have you sorted your inventory? Sometimes you will have multiple small stacks of the same item. You can collect these stacks together easily by double tapping on the item. This will collect all like items into a single stack, and may even free up a slot for more inventory!

5 LLAMA CARAVAN

Pack animals are a great way of maximising inventory space. Loading them with chests and steering them with leads, you can travel with a caravan of llamas carrying all your items. When mining for resources, attach the leads to a fence and the llamas will wait for your return. Just make sure you don't lose one!

6 OUTPOSTS

Building outposts short distances from your base is a fantastic way to manage your inventory and block supplies. Connect your outposts to your main base with rails, and when you need to clear up inventory, send supplies back to your base on a minecart. Use hoppers to automatically empty and store the contents so they're ready when you return.

CRAFTING EXPERT

Attention brave hero! Crisis has struck. The illagers have found the master recipe book and destroyed many of the recipes it contained. Throughout the realm, chaos brews as crafting tables produce broken and useless items. The recipe book needs to be repaired! Can you piece it back together?

WHAT'S THE RECIPE?

Match the items below to the recipes that make them — only four are needed!

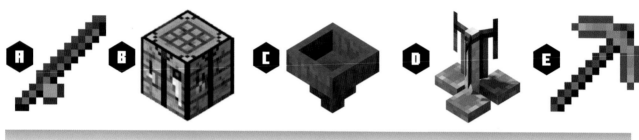

1 MY ANSWER

2 MY ANSWER

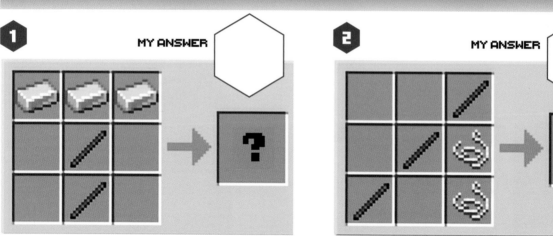

3 MY ANSWER

4 MY ANSWER

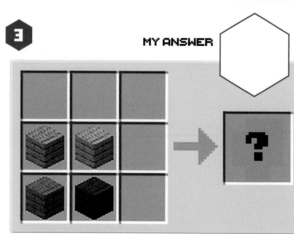

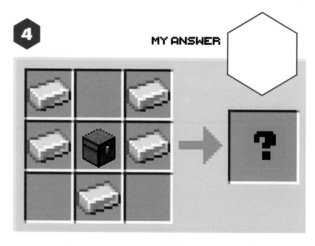

THE MISSING INGREDIENT

Match the missing ingredients to their recipes – there's one extra!

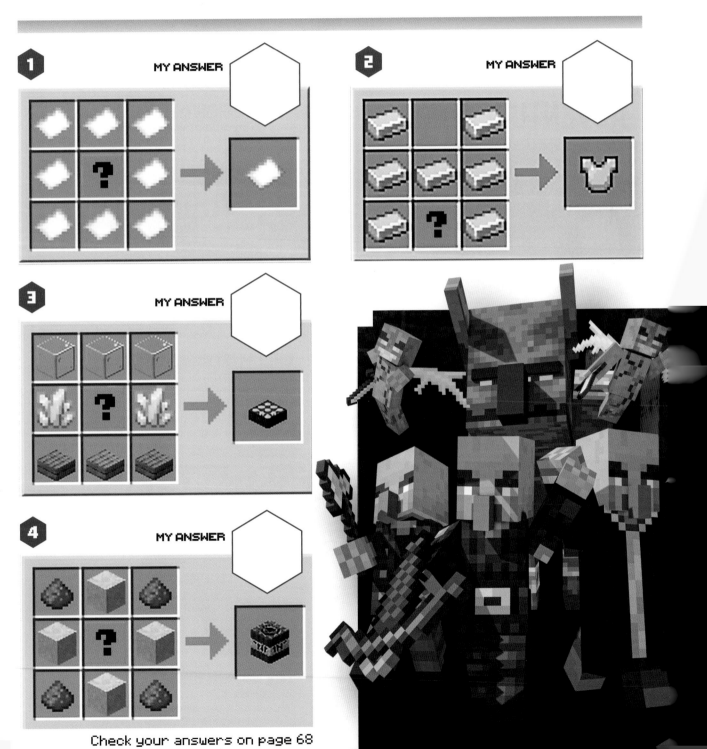

Check your answers on page 68

MARKETPLACE

We all need a change of scenery now and then, which is why it's such a lot of fun to discover new adventure maps and game types to play, or resource packs that will change up your worlds. There's so much to discover in the Minecraft Marketplace – here's a selection of some of the best the community has to offer!

 ## ADVENTURE MAPS

Download these cool Adventure Maps to add whole new experiences to enjoy solo or with friends!

ESCAPE THE HORROR HOUSE
BY PIXELONEUP

Yikes! This adventure is only for the bravest Minecrafters. You're trapped in the world's creepiest mansion and in order to escape you'll need to solve puzzles, pull off perfect parkour and battle oodles of monsters!

DREAM ISLAND: MADEIRA
BY PIXELBIESTER

Not every adventure needs to be stressful! Download this gorgeous interactive map and explore by land, sea and air to discover hidden secrets. Talk to the townsfolk, train and play with your dog, or decorate your new home. Chill out!

RAINFOREST WILDLIFE EXPLORERS
BY EVERBLOOM GAMES

This is the perfect adventure for nature lovers. Journey into a tropical rainforest with your camera to track down and photograph 20 completely new animal mobs. Slither with snakes and get snappy with crocodiles!

THE HUMAN BODY
BY GOE-CRAFT

This one is for everybody who loves gross science! This biological bonanza will take you on a stroll through the intestines, to all the major squishy organs and even on a wild minecart ride through a pumping bloodstream.

TEXTURE PACKS

Tired of the seeing same blocks? Here are some awesome texture packs to refresh your style!

MODERN CITY
BY GOE-CRAFT

This is a must-have for anyone building their own urban environment. Whether you want to craft towering office blocks or just dress up in smart suits, this texture pack will transform Minecraft's natural biomes into a concrete jungle.

TALES OF JOBUTARA KINGDOMS
BY PATHWAY STUDIOS

Give your world a complete, colourful fantasy makeover with this super-cool texture pack that even comes with its own custom user interface, stunning new block designs and loads of new villager skins.

CARTOON CRAFT
BY GOE-CRAFT

As well as adding a bright and cheerful new style to all the block types, this texture pack gives characters and mobs wacky cartoon faces! Even the scariest mob looks goofy and adorable – but watch out, they're still hostile mobs!

CLARITY
BY PATHWAY STUDIOS

Adding more detail and higher resolution to all the default textures and blocks, this is the pack to choose if you want to give your worlds a more realistic appearance. Even the most basic biome looks gorgeous with this!

SUPER RETRO
BY 4J STUDIOS

Maybe you don't want more detail? Maybe you'd like to see what Minecraft looks like with a simple retro style? This pack gives everything a chunky pixel look, so you can pretend you're inside a 1980s arcade game!

STAR ODYSSEY: BEYOND SPACE
BY ODD BLOCK

Attention all sci-fi fans! This complete cosmic makeover not only makes it easy to create alien worlds and moonbases, it also adds a host of weird alien creatures, zappy futuristic sound effects and completely new music.

MARKETPLACE

SURVIVAL PACKS

Add some extra wow factor to your Survival Mode games with these crazy custom spawn locations!

NETHER SECRET BASE
BY GOE-CRAFT

Ever fancied setting up home on the shores of a red-hot lava lake? This amazing ready-made HQ is full of cool features and unique redstone contraptions to add extra excitement to your Nether adventures.

SHELL KINGDOM
BY BLOCKLAB STUDIOS

Even Poseidon would be jealous of this massive ocean kingdom, complete with coral castles, hidden treasure and all-new creatures to tame or battle! Gather your friends and get ready to make a splash!

UNICORNS
BY NITRIC CONCEPTS

What's better than unicorns? Baby unicorns! You get both in this candy-coloured world, along with wizards and a rainbow castle. Oh, and did I forget to mention that the unicorns can fly? And you can ride them? Magic!

HOLLOW HILL
BY DRAGNOZ

One of the coolest packs we've seen, this download gives you a whole village to play with. What's so weird about that? The village is built on the inside of a giant spherical hill and features houses on the ceiling. Weird!

CRAFTABLE HOUSES
BY CUBED CREATIONS

How's this for a clever idea? This pack adds loads of unique crafting recipes, including complete buildings like a windmill, treehouse and a spooky witch's tower! Get out there, gather the materials and get crafting!

MASH-UPS

Discover new themes and characters with these great mash-up packs!

WACKY WEST
BY TEAM VISIONARY

Saddle up, cowpoke! You're off to the Wild West with this pack, featuring western character skins, a whole frontier town to start your adventure and even a few new animal mobs to encounter. Head out west to discover pastures new!

SKY UPGRADE
BY MYTHICUS

Take flight to a land of floating islands in the sky with this mega mash-up pack, which adds over 30 new skins and 50 new mobs. Discover all of the 40 flying villages, each with quests from villagers who need you to rebuild their homes. Up, up and away!

MONSTER SCHOOL
BY TEAM VISIONARY

Oh, no! Your friends have all been turned into monsters and evil forces have taken over your school! Who you gonna call? Er, you actually. You'd better get to work saving the day by tackling four beastly boss fights! Will you lift the curse and free your friends?

NINJA MASH-UP
BY EVERBLOOM GAMES

Put your black pyjamas on! It's over to Japan for this pack, which offers an entire 19th century town to explore. Join the fun as you take part in rooftop grapple hook races and battle mobs in the martial arts dojo.

NEON CITY
BY GOE-CRAFT

Jet off to a funky future in a sci-fi city crammed with working gadgets and vehicles, quests and mysteries, and best of all – robots! The neon blue and pink lighting gives it a unique feel, so go on – glow for it!

SEARCH & FIND: CAVES

All the excitement of new caves has caused a stir among the community. Players have crowded into caves all across the Overworld, eager to explore and discover. Everyone is having fun – except Scarlet. She has lost her pet wolf Luna. Can you help Scarlet find her? See if you can find all the missing mobs.

Tick the box as you find each of the missing mobs.

Check your answers on p68.

FRAGMENTS OF HISTORY

Little is known about the structures in the Overworld. Who built them? And why? Bear is determined to uncover the history of the past. Can you help him solve this age-old puzzle? Put your puzzle-solving skills to the test with this fragmented image.

INSTRUCTIONS

On this page are 11 puzzle pieces. Your challenge is to place 8 of the missing pieces in the correct slots on the picture on the opposite page. Write the number of each piece in the correct box.

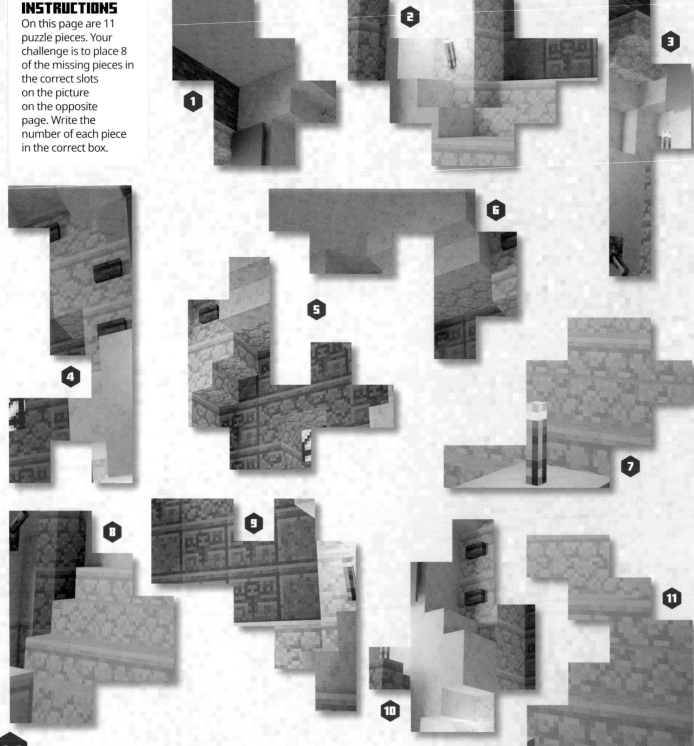

44

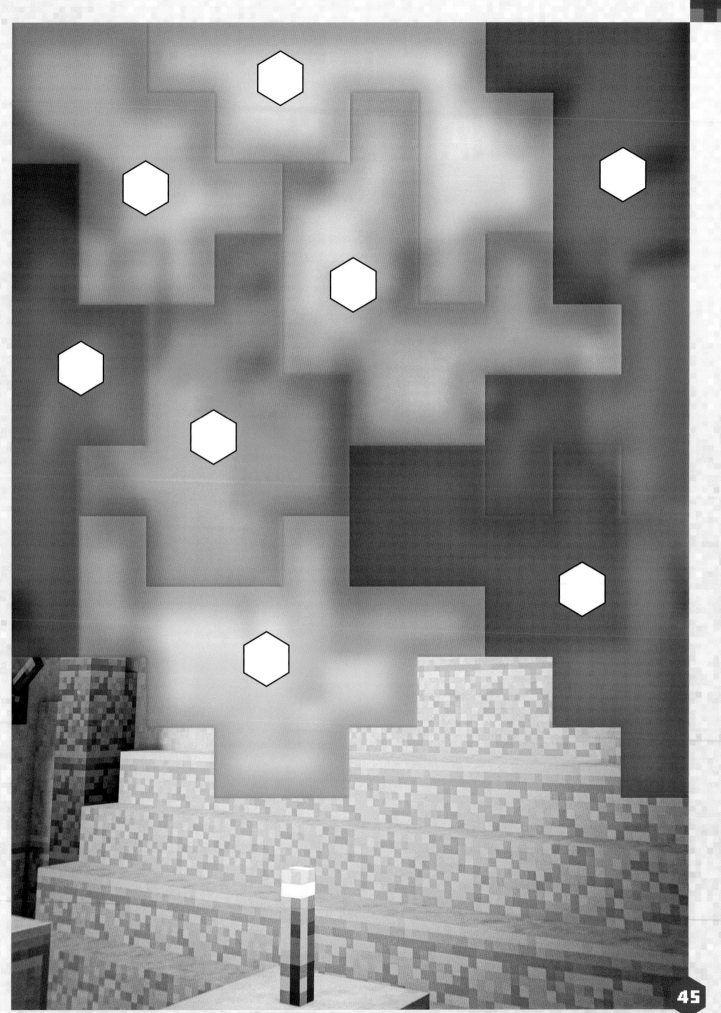

Check the answer on page 68

WORKSHOP BUILD CHALLENGE

BUILDING
WITH SPARKS

Construction projects take players all across the Overworld. Every location poses it's own unique challenges, as players are subjected to all manner of living conditions. When starting a new major build, it's important to have all the resources you need to hand. This field workshop will have you ready to take on any task.

HOME FROM HOME
If you're far away from your main base, changing your respawn location can save a lot of travel time. Place a bed in the workshop and use it to save your respawn location.

FIELD WORKSHOP STRUCTURE

🕐 **0.5 HRS**   ⬢⬢◯◯ **EASY**

Field workshops are temporary structures used while completing a major construction. They should be built from readily available blocks, like wood, so you can save your rare blocks for the main structure.

BUILD TIP

Build your field workshop near the construction site and be sure to include utility blocks like a crafting table. You'll likely need them to craft lots of block variants to complete your build.

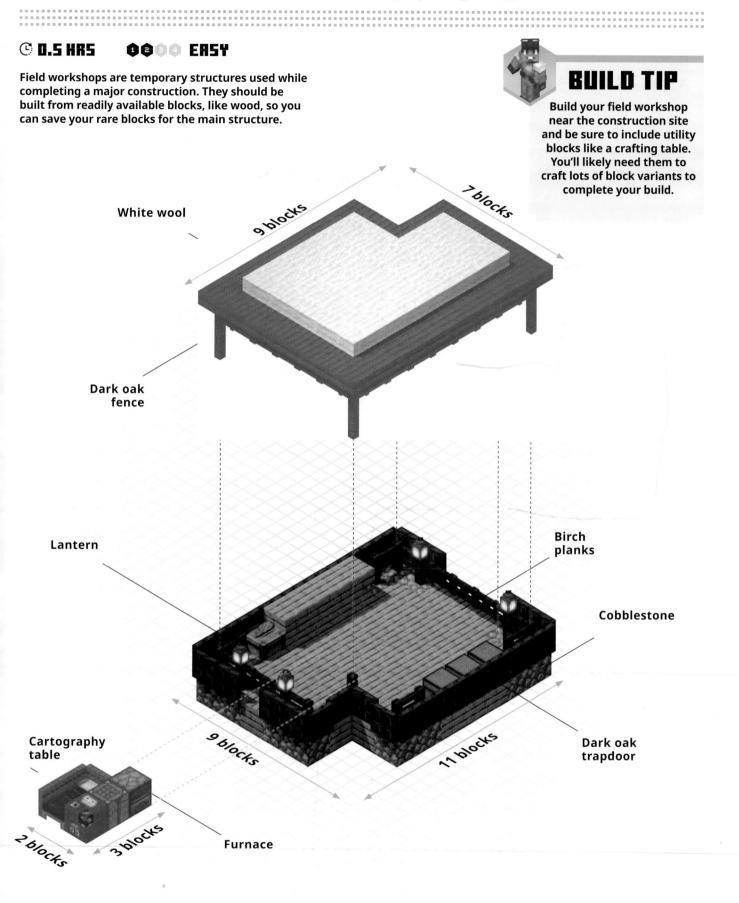

White wool

9 blocks

7 blocks

Dark oak fence

Lantern

Birch planks

Cobblestone

Cartography table

9 blocks

11 blocks

Dark oak trapdoor

2 blocks

3 blocks

Furnace

MINECRAFT DUNGEONS

EXPERT GUIDE WITH SCOUT

If you're looking for constant excitement, *Minecraft Dungeons* is the place to be. The dungeon crawler saw the addition of new characters to meet, weapons to find and – yikes – dangerous mobs and bosses to battle! Check out the latest dungeons, Jungle Awakens, Creeping Winter and Flames of the Nether!

MEET THE BLACKSMITH!

Got a fave weapon that you want to power up? Rescue the Blacksmith from the Redstone Mines and he'll set up shop in your camp. Pay him a visit, slip him some gold and he'll make your best weapons and armour even better!

LUXURY DEALS!

Just look at this fancy fellow – it's the Luxury Merchant! First you need to find them in Cacti Canyon and then unlock more of their wares by defeating bosses. They stock expensive high-level items that come loaded with enchantments, so save up and treat yourself!

ANCIENT HUNTS

Looking for the best gear in the game? Take your equipment and enchantment points and turn them into special missions for a chance to win some gilded gear. Choose wisely! Once you start a mission, there's no way of getting your kit back. High risk, high reward.

APOCALYPSE WHEN?

So you've finished all the missions, then beaten them again at Apocalypse difficulty. Reckon that's the end of the game? Nope! There's now Apocalypse Plus, which raises the challenge even higher but allows for even more levelling up. Strictly for expert players, this is the ultimate test!

FACE THE TRIALS!

Ready for a unique challenge? Then check out the Daily Trials! These are available from the Mission Select screen and require you to replay levels under special conditions on high difficulty settings. Reach the end and you'll earn an Obsidian Chest containing a Rare or Unique item. Bonus!

FLAMES OF THE NETHER

Turn up the heat! Do you have what it takes to face the wrath of the Nether's most dangerous mobs? This fiery new dungeon takes adventurers on six new missions to defeat mobs, find gear and recruit new companions.

CORRUPTED SEEDS

It's easy to get mobbed by, er, mobs in *Minecraft Dungeons* but this powerful Artifact from Jungle Awakens is great at clearing space around you. It summons deadly vines which grab and poison enemies, giving you a chance to catch your breath! Phew!

PSST, TOP SECRET!

Did you know there's a secret bonus stage in *Minecraft Dungeons*? It's true! I promised the Arch-Illager I wouldn't spoil the surprise but after beating Obsidian Pinnacle, maybe you should check out the church in your camp and start finding the hidden runes? Just a suggestion …

DUNGEONS SPOTLIGHT

JUNGLE AWAKENS

This steamy and perilous island is full of new leafy mobs that will test even the toughest warriors. Here's the lowdown on what to look out for on your quest!

WHISPERER

Beware this leafy foe! Up close it will whip you with its branches, and at a distance it will summon vines to ensnare or poison you.

LEAPLEAF

It might look like a pretty shrub but don't underestimate the leaper! It can jump a long distance and its shockwave does a lot of damage!

PANDA PLATEAU

This hidden area only spawns if you've uncovered all the secrets in Dingy Jungle. When crossing the canyon, head across the rope bridge rather than to the mission objective. Pass the statue and – with luck – the Plateau entrance won't be far away!

CREEPING WINTER

Wrap up warm if you want to survive in this frozen wilderness filled with icy enemies. Your goal is to reach the Lone Fortress but it won't be easy ...

WRETCHED WRAITH

Watch out for this terrifying boss that attacks with projectiles, teleports around and summons smaller mobs to help defeat you. It's snow joke!

FROZEN ZOMBIE

Think you know zombies? Think again! This chilly variation on a classic mob will throw snowballs and inflict freeze damage, slowing you down!

LOST SETTLEMENT

You'll need to explore Frozen Fjord to find this secret area when it spawns. Make your way through a creepy abandoned camp and battle the fiendish Illusioner!

WINTER'S TOUCH

This powerful new bow can be found in Frozen Fjord or Lost Settlement and can fire up to three arrows at a time when fully charged, each dealing cold damage.

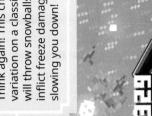

CHALLENGE
ESCAPE THE MAZE

The Arch-Illager is defeated and the Orb of Dominance shattered. Fragments have scattered, lost in dungeons throughout the land. Bear has set out to find them, exploring dungeons as he goes, but has been stopped in his tracks by this maze. Can you solve the puzzle and help Bear continue his quest?

CHALLENGE TIME WITH BEAR

START

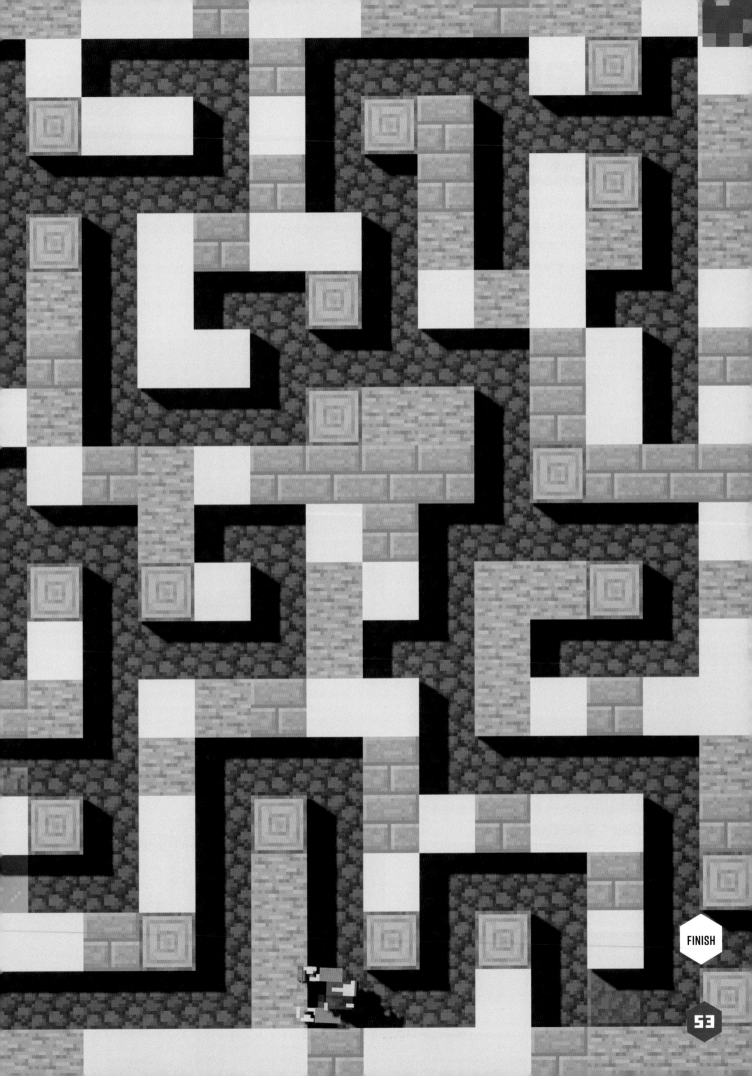

FINISH

MINECRAFT IN THE CLASSROOM

EDUCATION WITH MONTY

As well as the millions of players around the world using Minecraft to explore, build and craft, the Education Edition has been busy getting involved in some amazing projects to inspire students and keep people connected. Here are just some of the ways Minecraft has been changing the real world recently!

GLOBAL BUILD CHAMPIONSHIP

At the end of 2020, Minecrafters were offered the chance to take part in the first ever Global Build Challenge. Teams were challenged with designing new ways in which humans and wildlife can live together harmoniously!

URBAN GIRLS MOVEMENT

In Botkyrka, Sweden, a group of female students used Minecraft to redesign public areas of their town to make them safer and more accessible. Their idea for cube-shaped activity spaces was turned into real life structures. Using cubes to build with? Crazy!

MINECRAFT CAMP EXPERIENCE

Park University in Missouri, USA, has been running special Minecraft camps during school holidays. Participants explored the famous Oregon Trail and set sail in pirate ships. Best of all, they learned how to use coding to make it rain chickens! How egg-citing!

GOOD TROUBLE

A TIME OF CHANGE

Recent years have seen a lot of social unrest, with movements such as Black Lives Matter in the headlines. Minecraft Education has been helping people young and old understand and explore the subject of social justice through a series of interactive lessons based on the idea of "good trouble".

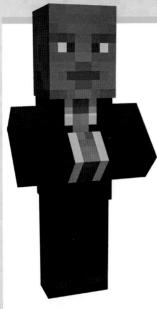

GOOD TROUBLE?

That's what US congressman John Lewis called it when people throughout history have had to make some noise to change and challenge unfair situations.

A MODERN HERO

You'll get to meet heroes both new and old, such as Malala Yousafzai, the Pakistani school girl who risked her life to help other girls get an education.

JOURNEY THROUGH TIME

Students can follow John Lewis back to the Civil Rights movement he helped lead in the 1960s with Dr. Martin Luther King Jr., and meet to other famous leaders like Nelson Mandela, Mahatma Gandhi and suffragette Emmeline Pankhurst all the way back in the 1900s!

NETHER BUILD CHALLENGE

BUILDING
WITH SPARKS

Step into the portal and travel to a fiery dimension – the Nether. Visiting the Nether is a perilous undertaking few adventurers will risk, no matter how valuable the reward. Will you attempt to breach this frontier and lay claim to the prizes it holds? Use the guide below to establish a foothold in this hostile land.

1 PORTAL TO THE NETHER

To travel to the Nether dimension, you need an obsidian portal. You can build a portal by placing obsidian blocks in a rectangular shape and activate it using a flint and steel. Alternatively, search the Overworld for a ruined portal and repair it to reach the Nether.

2 EXPLORE

With your sword and shield at the ready, take your first step into the Nether. This is a hostile land, so keep an eye on the piglins and hoglins that step too close. The first task at hand is to find a location for your base – search around for a nearby crimson forest.

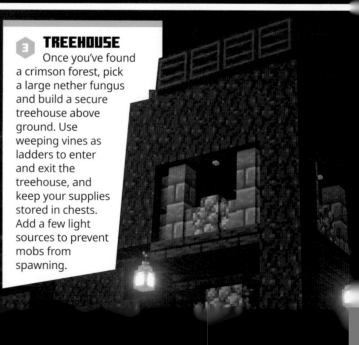

3 TREEHOUSE

Once you've found a crimson forest, pick a large nether fungus and build a secure treehouse above ground. Use weeping vines as ladders to enter and exit the treehouse, and keep your supplies stored in chests. Add a few light sources to prevent mobs from spawning.

FOOD SOURCE

5 You can breed and farm hoglins in the Nether using crimson fungi. Build a pen to contain the hoglins and breed them for food. Watch out! Hoglins are hostile and will attack you if you get too close. Barriers are a must!

RESPAWN LOCATION

4 Next, save your location with a respawn anchor. Do NOT try to sleep in a bed – it will explode! Instead, search the surrounding area for glowstone and crying obsidian, and collect them to craft a respawn anchor. Use glowstone to charge the respawn anchor, and when it's charged, use it to save your location.

DEFENCE

6 Piglins love gold and, by extension, players that wear gold. Grab your pickaxe and search for nether gold ore to mine. Keep mining until you have enough gold nuggets to create some armour. Wearing a piece of golden equipment will stop piglins from attacking you.

STRIDERS

7 The Nether is filled with lakes of lava. Wouldn't it be great if you could walk across them without getting hurt? It turns out you can! Well not you, but your striders can! Mount a strider and use warped fungus on a stick to lead it around.

NETHER BUILD CHALLENGE

BUILDING
WITH SPARKS

RESPAWN ANCHOR

Respawn anchors must be charged with glowstone to save a player's respawn location. Respawn anchors are crafted with zero charges and can have a maximum of four charges. Their charges can be depleted, and if you have no charges, you will respawn in the Overworld.

RESPAWN ANCHOR CHAMBER

🕒 **0.5 HRS** ●●○○ **EASY**

Respawning without any equipment will leave you vulnerable to piglin attacks, so make sure you build your respawn anchor in a safe space. This chamber will keep you protected from nearby mobs when you respawn.

BUILD TIP

Place a chest with emergency equipment near the respawn anchor. The Nether is a hostile place, and you never know when a piglin is nearby.

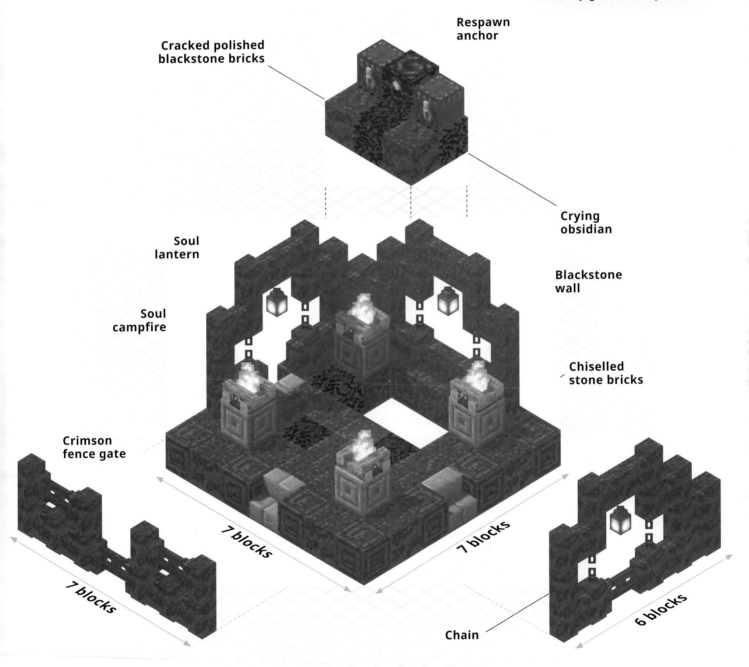

Cracked polished blackstone bricks

Respawn anchor

Crying obsidian

Soul lantern

Blackstone wall

Soul campfire

Chiselled stone bricks

Crimson fence gate

7 blocks

7 blocks

7 blocks

Chain

6 blocks

CHARACTER CREATOR

Alex and Steve may be two of the most recognisable Minecrafters out there – but they're far from the most fashionable. Since the release of the character creator in Bedrock Edition, players have been churning out countless unique outfits for their characters. Have you customised your character skin yet?

EXPERT GUIDE WITH MONTY

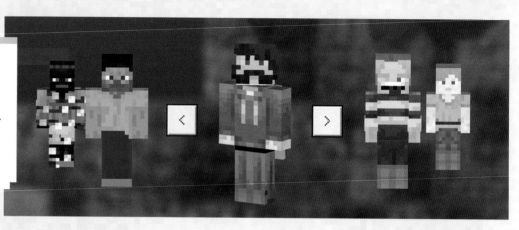

CHARACTER CREATOR

Character creator is a feature in Bedrock Edition that allows players to customise their appearance with cosmetic items. You can have up to five saved outfits and can choose between them via the character profile button on the main menu.

COSMETICS

There are hundreds of cosmetics to customise your avatar with, from gardening aprons to chicken arms. There are eight different categories, like top, bottom and footwear, giving you endless ways to make your character unique. Have a browse before picking your favourites.

BODY

Minecraft is a game for all, and as such, avatars can be customised to represent everyone. Choose between eight adjustable options such as face, arms, legs and body to create the character you wish. This is all purely cosmetic though – you'll still be the same Minecrafter in game as when you started.

COLLECTOR'S CLOTHING

Did you know there are lots of exclusive outfits that can only be unlocked as a reward? They can be earned at Minecraft events, as competition prizes and even for participation in online events. Look for these events to snag some cool kit!

STYLES

From party dresses to camo pants, there are lots of cosmetics to choose from to create your style. Alternatively, you can even create and upload your very own skins into the game. No matter what your style is, you're free to express yourself in you own way.

HEADGEAR

Many of these can be unlocked via achievements.

FACE ITEM

Whether you're looking for a disguise or some chunky sunglasses.

OUTERWEAR

Gadgets, knickknacks, cloaks, the list goes on and on!

BACK ITEM

Bunny tails, nutcracker keys, fairy wings, whatever you like!

TOP

The most visible cosmetic, this will be your first impression on other players.

GLOVES

From golfing to boxing, there's something for every occasion.

BOTTOM

Pants, trousers, shorts, skirts – all the options to make you feel like you.

READY FOR ACTION

If you see a player sporting this stupendous attire, you'll recognise them for the hero they are. From the camouflage green to health heart red, the Hero's outfit is inspired by adventure. You'll have to look but not touch – this outfit was an exclusive reward from *Minecraft Earth*.

FOOTWEAR

Shoes, sneakers, scandals ... and flower pots? Yet no clogs. Hmm.

MINECRAFT MASTER

Do you feel like you can accomplish anything in Minecraft? Let's find out! Create your very own game filled with in-game activities and challenge your friends to play. To win, a player must complete five tasks in any horizontal, vertical or diagonal row. The first to complete a row is crowned Minecraft Master.

CHALLENGE TIME WITH SCOUT

YOU WILL NEED
- Ruler
- Pencil
- 4 sheets of paper

1 DRAW YOUR PLAYING CARDS

Using the ruler and pencil, draw a 4x4 block grid on each sheet of paper. Don't worry if you can't draw block shapes, simple squares or circles will do.

2 PICK YOUR TASKS

Create lists of in-game tasks for players to complete. You can give everyone the same tasks, or, for a tougher challenge, you can create unique tasks for each card. We've got you started below.

1 Tame a wolf

2 Find a diamond

3 Create an iron golem

4 Bake a cake

5 Reach the End

6 Find a village

7 Build a house

8 Grow a pumpkin

9 Place a cactus in a flowerpot

10 Complete a map

11 Find a saddle

12 Play music

13 Find a stronghold

14 Capture a zombie

15 Trade for an emerald

16 ....

17 ....

18 ....

19 ....

20 ....

21 ....

22 ....

23 ....

24 ....

25 ....

26 ....

27 ....

28 ....

29 ....

30 ....

Activity continues on page 65

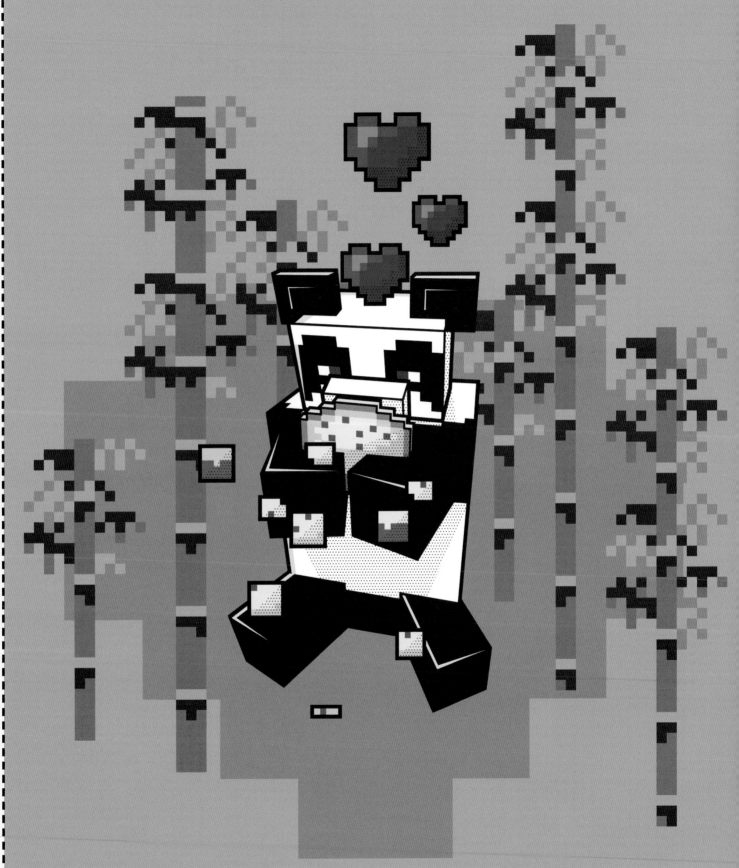

MINECRAFT

Activity continued from page 62

3 CREATE THE PLAYING CARDS

Start filling out the cards with all your tasks. If each of your cards has the same tasks, try mixing up the tasks up so that each vertical, horizontal and diagonal lines are unique.

MINECRAFT
MASTER

5   7   10   16

1   8   14   12

15   2   6   9

13   8   3   4

4 INVITE YOUR FRIENDS

It's time to invite three of your friends to play. Create a new server, invite your friends to join you and send them their playing cards. When a player has finished, they must show they've completed a row of tasks.

MINECRAFT
MASTER

~~5~~   7   10   16

1   ~~8~~   14   12

15   2   ~~6~~   9

13   8   3   ~~4~~

CAMPFIRE TALES

You're amazing! Yes, you! In fact, the whole Minecraft community is full of awesome, inspiring people doing incredible things, and it's always exciting to see what they get up to. Each year we get dozens of stories about the fantastic things happening in Minecraft, and here are some of our recent faves!

EXPERT GUIDE
WITH SPARKS

THE WHOLE WIDE WORLD!

Over the years we've seen people building towns, cities, even entire countries. What's next? The whole world, obviously! The Build The Earth Project is exactly what it sounds like – over 100,000 players working together to create an accurate scale replica of the actual planet we're all sitting on right now, down to the individual streets and buildings! There are over 3000 build teams all working on their own little bit of the world, so head to buildtheearth. net if you want to join in!

SEED DETECTIVES!

Do you recognise this picture? If you've been playing Java Edition, you should do – it's the default image shown when you're picking a texture pack or server. But where is it and can you go there? A group of enterprising fans have finally worked it out using AI software to locate which of the game's 281 trillion possible seed worlds it comes from. To visit this iconic scene, load Java version Alpha 1.2.2a and enter seed 3257840388504953787, coordinates x=49, z=0.

SAVE THE ALIENS!

We love to showcase ambitious and imaginative build projects, and this dazzling construction definitely fits the bill! It's called Hive City and creator Jordan, a popular UK Minecrafter, has even come up with a whole story to explain his design, inspired by real world conservation efforts. It's set in the year 3221, when humankind has encountered alien species. Discovering that some aliens are endangered, Hive City is built to recreate their environments and keep them safe. A brilliant, heart-warming story and an amazing build project!

YOU'LL DIG THIS!

Spending more time at home gave players the chance to create amazing builds, and we particularly love this project from archaeologist Dr Ben Edwards and his daughter Bella. They put their time to great use and recreated the prehistoric Bryn Celli Ddu site in Minecraft. This ancient tomb is believed to be around 5000 years old and thanks to Ben and Bella, we can now explore the inside from the comfort of our homes using Minecraft, with useful signposts explaining what we can see every step of the way. Very cool! Nice work, Ben and Bella!

GOODBYE

Oh, so *that's* what happened in 2021! You know, it only makes me more excited for what's to come next year. Speaking of which ... we'll have lots more amazing things to share over the coming months, promise.

Thanks for playing!

Alex Wiltshire
Mojang Studios

ANSWERS

18-19

45

36

1 - E	3 - B
2 - A	4 - C

37

1 - B	3 - E
2 - C	4 - A

42-43

52-53